WHERE'S HELLO KITTY?
Fashion Star

First published in the UK by HarperCollins Children's Books in 2012
3 5 7 9 10 8 6 4 2
ISBN: 978-0-00-748758-5

HarperCollins *Children's Books*

How to play

Hello Kitty is a super-stylish fashion star. In fact lots of girls are trying to look as good as she does. So it's no wonder it can be very difficult to spot Hello Kitty in a crowd these days. Can you spot the real Hello Kitty in every scene, using the picture at the top as a guide?

It's more difficult than you might think; lots of girls look very similar to Hello Kitty and have just one or two small differences. Remember though, there's only one Hello Kitty!

There are lots of other fun activities inside to keep you entertained.

As well as Hello Kitty and Mimmy, you'll also find Hello Kitty's friends in each crowd. Can you spot them all in every scene?

Dear Daniel

Thomas

Fifi

Tippy

Jodie

Moley

Rory

Mimmy

Joey

Tracy

Timmy and Tammy

Where's Hello Kitty?

Hello Kitty is always in demand for photo shoots. Today she's on her way to meet a famous photographer. Look how many girls have turned up.

FASHION PHOTO SHOOT

Where's Hello Kitty?

Hello Kitty loves to dress in stylish outfits and have her photo taken.

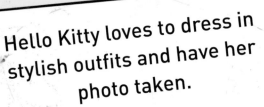

Suitcase Jumble

Hello Kitty is packing for a photo shoot at the beach. Can you help her to pack? Circle all the things she will need.

Where's Hello Kitty?

Hello Kitty has headed to her dance studio to practise her routine. She loves to keep fit and healthy.

Where's Hello Kitty?

Hello Kitty fits in some lovely, relaxing pampering time.

STEAM ROOM
& SAUNA

Create an Outfit

Hello Kitty loves experimenting with new looks. Can you draw her a super-stylish outfit? Don't forget to add a fabulous handbag too.

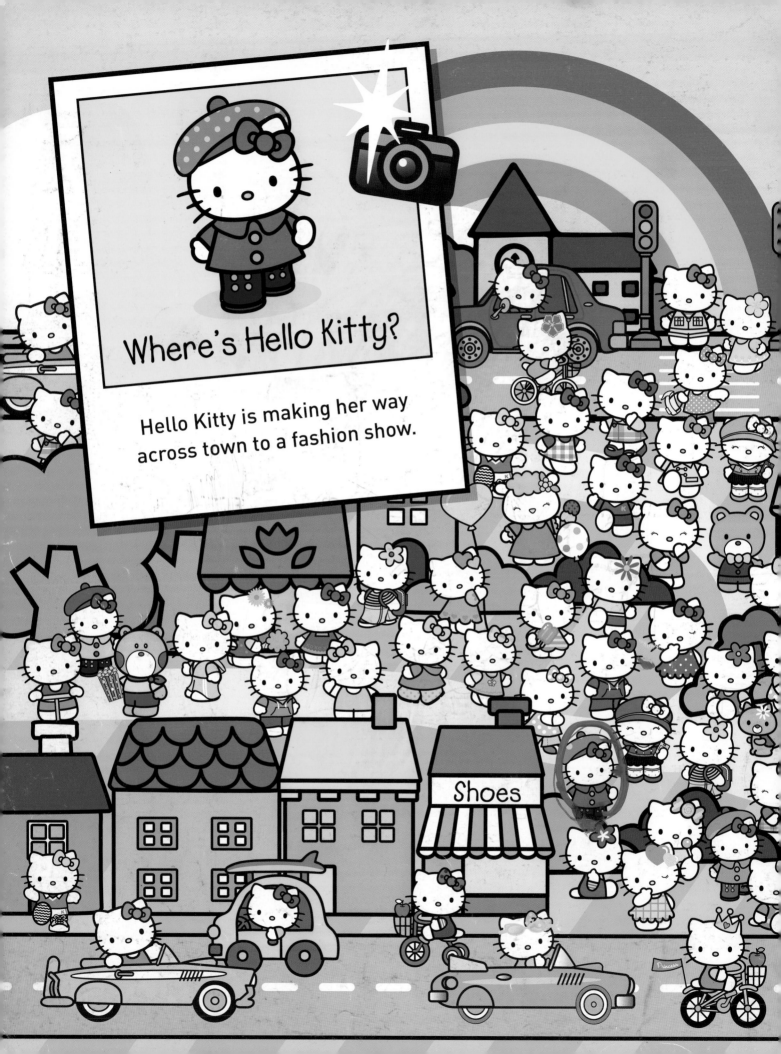

Where's Hello Kitty?

Hello Kitty is making her way across town to a fashion show.

City Maze

Hello Kitty has to find her way through the city to the show. Help to guide her through the maze – and hurry! She can't be late.

Start
Here or here

Finish
••••••▶

Where's Hello Kitty?

Hello Kitty has to fly to another country for a fashion shoot. Crowds of fans have gathered at the airport.

X-RAY

X-RAY

T-shirt Fun

Hello Kitty is thinking of starting her very own fashion range. She needs to choose some designs. Can you help her by colouring in these funky T-shirts?

Where's Hello Kitty?

Hello Kitty still makes sure she keeps up with her studies. She's a popular student!

Where's Hello Kitty?

Fabulous photographs of Hello Kitty have been published in a fashion magazine. There are lots of other lookalike girls.

Hello... Hello Kitty

Fashion Star Hello Kitty wowed on the catwalk when the beautiful and talented icon took part in a fashion show.

Designer Diva

Can you help Hello Kitty set out in style by designing your own fabulous range of accessories?

Stylish sneakers

Show-stopping jewels

Sassy sun hat

Super shades

Beautiful beach bag

Where's Hello Kitty?

Hello Kitty has been invited to a very glamorous party. She looks every inch the fashion star in her stunning outfit.

Checklist

Hello Kitty still needs your help. There's one lost item somewhere in the crowd on each page. Can you find them all? Search all the scenes until you have found every item.

Hello Kitty ✕

Pink sunglasses

A pink necklace

A purple mirror

A note pad and pencil

A green handbag

A stripy bow

Hello Kitty's favourite perfume

A flowery hat